Jumpstarting Your Inner Novelist

JE Thompson

and

Dennis DeRose

"Keep Writing

Keep Believing

Never Give Up On Your Dreams!"

From The Editor's Desk

I became acquainted with Julius as he was completing the third book of his "Pilgrim" trilogy, The Ghost of Atlanta. I was excited when he asked me to edit this book; I had a good feeling about him and his work. I talked to him at length about the book and over time we became a writing team, a writer and an editor working together to make his book the best it could be.

Our close working relationship, riddled with constant give-and-take communication, paid off when The Ghost of Atlanta won the Readers Favorite gold award for best fiction. During that time, Julius asked me to re-edit the first two books in the trilogy, A Brownstone in Brooklyn and Philly Style and Philly Profile. I did that while vacationing in Australia. About one year after that, Julius requested that I edit his new YA fiction, Purple Phantoms, a paranormal fiction about two things that he loves , basketball and his students. The title was later changed to Phantoms of Rockwood. I eagerly await the chance to edit his fifth novel, Stormy Winds.

My wife, Carla, and I had the privilege to meet Julius at a writer's conference in Georgia, not too far from Atlanta. At first glance, I saw a man in a nice suit, but later I realized he was much more than that. This meeting cemented a friendship. We had our picture taken together; he was holding a copy of Ghost in his hand. Later, I looked at that photo and I saw a man beaming with pride.

I am honored to have been asked to write this introduction to Julius' guide to writing a successful novel. He has even asked me to write a section about editing and good grammar, two very important necessities that can help make a book successful.

Now, grab something cool to drink, find a quiet place, sit down and relax, clear your mind and get ready to read Julius' tips and tricks about little things you can do to help make yourself a better writer. Julius and I hope you will enjoy this short read. Contact information for welcomed comments is located in the "About the Authors" section.

Editor and Co-author, Dennis De Rose

Musings, Thoughts and Goals for the Budding Author!

After teaching Creative Writing and Publishing at Evening at Emory University Writer's Studio for nine years and writing four published novels, including a national gold medal winner in the fiction genre, I decided to record my thoughts and ideas about creating successful novels and weave them into a practical guide for writers.

During my years at Evening at Emory, I helped students fine-tune their skills concerning all stages of the writing process: from first draft to day of publication. This guide, co-authored by my friend and editor, Dennis De Rose, will provide you with a set of tools to help you address issues such as developing captivating scenes, creating vivid descriptive specific details, living in the setting, editing and grammar and other crucial elements to help you write a potentially successful novel.

Best of Luck and God Bless

JE Thompson

Table of Contents

I.Dwayne Morris: A Former Emory Student's Perspective

"When I sat in a big, chilly classroom and heard this powerfully-built, swift talking man say that in four months, I will have written a novel, I thought, *he's crazy*. I'd been nibbling around, working with disjointed stories, random scenes, and one-dimensional characters for years and was lucky to cobble together a 4,000 word short story. I'd have to see it to believe it, a complete novel in four months.

Four months later, another student and I were laying out dozens of finished chapters on tables in that same refrigerated classroom. While doing this, that same swift-talking man, Julius Thompson, chuckled as he snapped photos of his graduates, each one beaming over their first completed novels. Seeing is believing."

---D.A. Morris

II.*More Testimonals*

"Julius' encouragement, thorough reviews of my work, and emphasis on discipline (setting a certain amount of time aside each day to write) contributed to my finishing novel (Essie in Progress)." --- **Marjorie Presten, author of a published novel: Essie in Progress**

=================

When I received Mary's email, inviting me to her book signing, it was a thrill to see someone I had helped achieve her dream. She wrote, "I thought you would like to know that one of your former students is now a published author...

"Your creative writing class I took at Emory three years ago was a great inspiration to crafting the art of writing. My first book was written last year over a period of six months.   Today, I am working on the next phase of my writing, a children's book that I plan to illustrate.**"---Mary Gilmartin, author of the published novel: Adventures with Easton**

=================

"I had an opportunity to take a creative writing class with Julius at Emory University. Julius is very passionate and dedicated to his work. Whether it in or outside of the class, he is always available to assist students with their journey to become successful writers." ---**Abdul Shaikh**

================

"For twenty years I had nothing but notebooks filled with random thoughts and grand ideas. Then Julius Thompson became my mentor. With his guidance I overcame my doubt and began to discover the story that was hidden in my head. His coaching and experience as an author helped me to write my first novel; it made it all the way to a publishers' desk. Now I'm using the skills I learned from him to structure new stories and craft my voice as I pursue my dream of publication."---**Robert Brunet**

================

"Julius Thompson was my Instructor at Emory. His techniques and tips on Novel Writing helped me become the author I am today!" **S.R. Johannes, author of the award-winning *Nature of Grace*teen series.**

III.One Writer's Journey to Writing Success!

Developing Confidence in your writing ability

Sometimes when I enter my writing area, a corner of my office, it seems that words will not come and the critic inside me attacks my creativity with the constant bombardment of negative thoughts.

Enough! *I say to myself*

Finally, I sit down, strike the letters on the keyboard and let the words energize each other as they create vivid word pictures that become vibrant mental images for my readers. I'm on my writing schedule and I believe in myself once more!

I wasn't always this confident in my writing ability.

I once listened to the "Rules Police" or "Peer Critics" and didn't believe enough to even look inside myself to come up with the courage to write a single line. I was scared, really scared, at one time in my life, but that was, many years ago, my high school days during the turbulent sixties.

What happened to help me develop confidence in my writing ability? Here's the fateful story.

It was a faithful fall day; I was a junior at Bushwick High, in Brooklyn, New York.

I was scared to express my thoughts, any thoughts, because of my rural southern background. During that time I learned to put my ego under a deep cover of quietness, otherwise my opinions brought retribution to my doorsteps.

Heck, I was even afraid to look people in the eye, thanks to the oppressive segregated atmosphere of small town early sixties Georgia. Self-Esteem and Self-Confidence were sorely lacking in my personality.

I knew I had an amazing ability to write, but my motivation and confidence were at a sub-zero level.

During my second year, at Bushwick, after moving from Statham, Georgia, population 300 and segregated, to Brooklyn, population 3,000,000 and integrated. I got up enough nerve to ask my English teacher and student council/general organization sponsor, Ms. Egan, a question. I knew if the answer was negative, all my hopes and dreams of becoming the next great novelist would be dashed.

I knocked hard on the door to her office, entered, and asked her straight out, "Can I be a writer?"

She stared at me for a few moments and then said, "Do It!"

I haven't looked back.

As a high school English teacher, I know how the power of positive or negative words can affect a student's life. What I learned that fall day in Brooklyn, I try to instill in my students today.

My writing Career:

***I have written articles for The New York times.

***I wrote for the Philadelphia Bulletin (receiving the National Sports Writing Award---for the third third best story in the United States in 1977)

***I wrote for the Atlanta Journal Constitution.

***I wrote for the Associated Press.

***I wrote for a national publication: Sports Scene Magazine

***I wrote for another   national publication: Parade Magazine

***Published Novels: A Brownstone in Brooklyn, Philly Style and Philly Profile, The Ghost of Atlanta, Phantoms of Rockwood and a work in progress, Stormy Winds,

***Georgia Author of the year nominee 2007: Philly Style and Philly Profile

***Georgia Author of the year nominee 2011: The Ghost of Atlanta

***2011 National Gold Medal Fiction Award Winner from Readers' Favorite for The Ghost of Atlanta!

Ms. Egan would be very proud of me!

Not bad for a scared little kid from the Bush Chapel Section of a small town in Georgia.

Just like my high school English teacher told me: "Do it!" I know you can.

IV.Authors must create their own Writing Style!

What kind of writer are you? What is your writing style?

If you are sensitive to critics' comments, the "Rules Police", experts that discuss this issue, with such aplomb that they intimidate, I suggest turn a deaf ear to this shrill commentary that says: *You must write in a certain style in order to be considered a worthy author.*

Stop thinking like that!

Your writing is created out of your personality. You must reach deep inside your creative self to find *out* how you will put words on paper.

I'm a "Conversational" writer...what does that mean? I write, as if, I'm having a wonderful conversation, over a glass of wine, with the reader. I'm telling a story and I want to capture the reader's attention, not with long flowery descriptions, but with simple sentences that build incredible word pictures using active verbs and creative adjectives.

Here is a good example is from my first novel, <u>A Brownstone in Brooklyn</u>,

I wanted to describe how a person's dreams may be answered, but dreams are fleeting they come and go in the blink of an eye. They never last, I want the reader to understand that if you don't change you will live in the past always trying to capture that same dream over and over again:

"The most special times in a person's life are not meant to last forever. They're like bubbles rising from a plastic ring dipped into a soapy solution. The soap bubbles rise, with the sun flashing brilliant colors, then bursts into a showery memory mist."

— J.E. Thompson, *A Brownstone in Brooklyn*

I wanted to create word pictures that captured this feeling of a fleeting moment in time.

Watching the Miss Marple series on PBS, based on Agatha Christie's books. I remember one episode episode particularly, it was based on In Bertram's Hotel, and Christie said, "The essence of life is change and we have to adjust and change."

I wanted to create this moment in my book, using my writing style, just like Agatha Christie created, using her style.

For example, I love the sixties, but I can't live in the sixties, but I must adjust to the music and the moments of the 21st Century.

I remember one moment that changed a nation. I remember exactly where I was when it was announced that President Kennedy had been shot. I was in gym class at Bushwick High in Brooklyn on a cool November Day in 1962. It is still fresh in my mind, the moment my gym teacher, Coach Diamond, told us the news of Kennedy's assignation. We were stunned. Some of us cried.

Now I must live in the rhythm of the 21st century with Hip Hop, Rap the threat of ISIS terrorism and other dominate themes. If I want to remain relevant in this present age, You must do the same or be buried by the past's minutia. Don't forget the past but DO not dwell on it.

My writing has always been crisp, with short sentences, just like F. Scott Fitzgerald (The Great Gatsby), Ernest Hemingway (The Old Man and the Sea), Zora Neale Hurston (Their Eyes were Watching God) and Walter Mosley (Devil in aa Blue Dress).

My style is not like that of Tony Morrison, William Faulkner and other authors that are expert in the use of long complex sentences.

That's their style.

Authors must take time to find a style with experimentation in different writing styles, their own unique style. May I suggest that you experiment with different writing styles *to see what fits you.*

I believe in what Polonius said to Hamlet, "To Thine own self be true."

Be true to yourself as you write and experiment.

Don't imitate, but create your own unique writing style.

Never listen to the "Rules Police."

I wish you much success as you find your writing style, one that will help you write fantastic novels.

V. How to Choose a Point of View in Your Novel?

How am I going to tell my story? Which Point of View (POV) should I use?

When I sit in front of my computer and start to pound the keyboard, I must decide on the point of view I want to use to tell my story! I swallow hard and try to figure out the "voice" in which to write my novel...so many choices!

What *are* the definitions of points of view?

Point of view is the way the author allows you to "see" and "hear" what's going on in the novel. Skillful authors can fix their readers' attention on exactly the right detail, opinion or emotion the author wants to emphasize by manipulating the point of view of the story. Literature provides us with lens through which readers look at the world.

***Point of view or POV pertains to who tells the story and how it is told. Point of View comes in three varieties: First-Person, Second-Person and Third-Person. First-Person point of view is used when a character narrates the story using words like I-Me-Mine-Mine-His-Her

The advantage of this point of view is that you get to hear the thoughts of the narrator and see the world depicted in the story through his/her eyes. A First-Person Example: To Kill A Mockingbird by Harper Lee. Second-person point of view is not common, the author directly uses like you or yours. Writers seldom speak directly to the reader. When you encounter this POV, please pay attention.

Second-person is distracting and hard to sustain in longer works of fiction. Refer to Bright Lights by Jay McInerney

Third-person POV is used by news reporters, outsiders looking at the action. The writer may choose third-person omniscient, in which the thoughts of every character are open to the reader...or third-person limited, in which the reader enters only one character's mind, either throughout the entire work or in a specific section.

Third-person limited differs from first person because the author's voice, not the characters, is what you hear in the descriptive passages. A good example of Third-Person is <u>Pride and Prejudice</u> by Jane Austen when you're reading a third-person selection, either limited or omniscient, you're watching the story unfold via an outsider.

Most writers choose this point of view. When choosing a point of view, ask yourself this question: *What serves the story best?* Hint--If you are stuck trying to pick a point of view, write paragraphs using the three points of view. Write the same paragraph three times, using a different POV each time and see which one works best. I hope this helps you in your quest. Feel free to ask me for help if you need it. POV is not easy to understand.

VI. Establish Setting Early in Your Novel

Where am I?

This is a question you DON'T want your readers to dwell on as they turn the pages of your novel.

Picking the setting of a novel is obviously a critical step.

You must craft a vivid realistic setting to act as a backdrop canvass in order for your characters to perform within it. This setting/sense of place must be credible.

When you read great works of fiction, you know immediately where and what time period you are in. For example, Walter Mosley puts you in early fifties' Los Angeles in Devil in a Blue Dress, Harper Lee sets you in the early twentieth century south in To Kill A Mockingbird and F. Scott Fitzgerald sets you in the roaring twenties within the setting of The Great Gatsby.

You must give your reader a sense of place. This will make it easier for your readers to exist in the "Fictional Dream" of your novel's world.

A great author once said: "Characters interact with setting/sense of place as if its' another character. The setting/sense of place will change the character. In a different sense of place the characters will be different."

When crafting your novel, ask yourself a couple of questions. What is the relationship of a particular setting to my novel's main characters? Can I imagine him/her/them in a different setting?

What happens in novels, when the protagonists (the leading character, hero, or heroine of a drama or other literary work) appear in a new setting—what does that have to do with what the book is about?

For example, one of my point of view characters, Andy Michael Pilgrim, lived, interacted and changed in the three novels of the trilogy.

In the progression of the trilogy, Andy's early adult life was shaped while growing up in Brooklyn, New York. After moving to Philadelphia, he was shocked while watching the influence of drugs and gangs destroy young people's lives, knowing that the environment was something that he had little or no control over. He felt helpless. Finally, returning to the town where he was raised, near Atlanta, Georgia, he was affected by the negative memories of his past.

The three cities acted like major characters forcing Andy to react as if he was confronting a living person in each novel.

As you craft your novel, ask yourself, *"Where does the action take place?"*

While reading your novel, the reader must learn pretty quickly during what place and time the story unfolds—in other words, where in time and space the story "is" set.

The setting is the backbone of your novel; it is the backbone upon which you will build a cast of dynamic characters. Research your setting so you can add very specific details, making your setting as realistic as possible. You must be very descriptive in your setting to pull the reader in, to keep people turning the pages and keep people reading your book.

When choosing the setting for your novel, ask yourself these questions:

1. What year is it?

2. *What city and/or town do my characters live in?*

3. *What is the weather like?*

4. *What season is it?*

5. *What type of architecture is found in my setting?*

6. *What can I do to paint a picture of the setting in the reader's mind?*

I hope these hints help you to create realistic settings for your novels or short stories.

VII.What is Stream of Consciousness in a Novel?

I was lounging on a couch on the outside deck of the Starbucks in Tucker, Georgia, enjoying a tall "Flat White" coffee. It was good and creamy...very good in fact! The sun was hot, but a crisp cool breeze washed over the deck and kept me alert as I read J.D. Sallinger's <u>The Catcher in the Rye.</u> The traffic on Highway 29 didn't distract me as I was involved in reading this classic novel<u>.</u>

A few minutes earlier, while buying my drink, the barrister smiled, noticing my book, and said, "I remember that book from high school a few years ago." I smiled and said, "So do I, many, many, many years ago in high school in Brooklyn.

We both laughed!

You might wonder why I referred back to my old Bushwick High reading list. There was a review I had read about a chapter in one of my novels. At first I was surprised, a little stunned, as I read the review a number of times: *"Fluid writing style. Plenty of concrete detail that defines the character and the street names of cities I'm not familiar with. I feel as if I'm witnessing Walter with binoculars from a distance. I know who he is, but it's not enough. Without some stream-of-consciousness I can't sympathize with his death. He's just an accident victim on the evening news."*

I leaned back and thought this reader didn't know or care about said character in my novel.

As I reread and concentrated on the review over and over, the words *"I know who he is, but it's not enough"* kept replaying in my mind. This is what a review is supposed to do for a writer; make him or her think.

Now, I am in the midst of writing a philosophical novel, <u>Stormy Winds</u>, this particular review is giving me food for thought about the concerning the development my characters, especially the lead character Justin Fleming,

I keep asking myself, *"What is "Stream of Consciousness" in a novel?*

Most people think Stream of Consciousness means: *"In literary criticism, stream of consciousness is a narrative mode that seeks to portray an individual's point of view by giving the written equivalent of the character's thought processes, either in a loose interior monologue, or in connection to his or her actions."* This is the answer from a dictionary.

While definitions are easy to recite, I ask myself *what does it mean and how do you make this writing technique work in a novel?*

After reading the review again, I realized I needed to find examples of Stream of Consciousness. Give me some examples of effective Stream of Consciousness in a successful book! I kept thinking the book that came to mind was <u>The Catcher in the Rye</u>. Well, I decided to read the book again to get a feel for this technique.

Since I didn't have a nice copy of the novel, I decided the book at my local Barnes & Nobel, in paperback, not in E-Book format. Paperbacks are easier for me to read and read again.

I'm reading this classic again, not as a dreaded high school English assignment, but as a present day author trying to learn something from an American Classic.

What is Stream of Consciousness?

***Is it a character's random thoughts that cruise through a person's mind?

***Is it a character's reaction to a developing situation?

*** *Is it a character going back in time and reacting to an event?*

*** *Is it a character musing about a future event?*

***Are you giving the reader insight into the character and why the person does what he does in the novel?*

Is it a book told strictly from the first person POV?

As I read <u>The Catcher in the Rye,</u> I'm observing how a great author uses this technique to help the reader "Know who the character is!"

A small excerpt from the novel:

"If you really want to hear about it, the first thing you'll probably want to know is where I was born and what my lousy childhood was like, and how my parents were occupied and all before they had me, and all that David Copperfield kind of crap, but I don't feel like going into it, if you want to know the truth.

The Catcher in the Rye
Holden Caulfield in Chapter 1, opening words of the book.

As I'm reading, I'm learning who Holden Caulfield is and what his personality is like. This will be, I've decided, a very informative reading adventure and a learning process for me.

The late afternoon sunlight creates a nice atmosphere while sitting on the deck of the Tucker Starbucks, as I carefully read each and every word, phrase and incident to figure out what "Stream of Consciousness" really means. For me, it is the thoughts of the character revealing the essence of the person.

One thing I've learned about the writing process is that you never stop learning. You must always have that thirst for knowledge and to improve your craft. This reading exercise encourages me to take the next step in crafting my best novel, <u>Stormy Winds;</u>

VII. **Building Characters: Fill Out a Character Resume!**

Plausible complex characters are crucial to successful storytelling. This involves the protagonist, the antagonist and a carnival of other minor characters.

The importance of character development was hammered home for me at the AJC-Decatur Book Festival, when New York Times best-seller Author, N. M. Kelby, did an impressive two-hour presentation on character development.

Think of any great book and the main character should pop into your mind: Pride and Prejudice: Elizabeth Bennett; The Great Gatsby: Nick Caraway; Janie Starks: Their Eyes Were Watching God; Janie Starks; To Kill a Mockingbird: Scout Finch; Devil in a Blue Dress: Easy Rawlins, etc.

Your Main Character:
1. Delivers your point of view to your readers.
2. Is identified forever with your book.
3. Must be memorable and creates lasting memories for your readers.

All of your characters should respond to their experiences by changing or by working hard to avoid changing. While they seek to carry out their agendas, run into conflicts, fail or succeed, and confront new problems, they will not stay the same.

If you want to write a successful novel, you must create a realistic group of characters to move your plot along.

How do you get to know your Characters?

You must create a character resume for your protagonist, your antagonist and a few of your minor characters.

Use a resume as if a character was applying for a job in your novel. You must complete a resume for your characters. This will give you the opportunity to get to know each of them.

While writing my fourth novel, Phantoms of Rockwood, I had to develop totally new characters; this is a YA fiction and was something I had never done before. So it was back to drawing board for me,

Before I even wrote a word of Phantoms of Rockwood I filled

out a resume for all the major characters. This helped me get to know all the people that would carry the storyline in the novel.

Will you use everything in a resume? No!

What you will learn is how your characters will react in certain stressful situations during critical moments in your book.

How can you put your characters in critical situations if you don't know their personalities?

You need to fill out a Character Resume to help find the answers.

I have a character resume form that I use for the protagonist, the antagonist and other minor characters.

From past experience, I've learned the importance of developing this resume, it contains many questions. You don't want to delve into your book and still not know what makes your characters tick.

Here is an example of a few of the items in the resume:

Character Name:
Address & Phone Number:
Date & Place of Birth:
Height/Weight/Physical Description:
Citizenship/Ethnic Origin:
Parents' Names & Occupations:

Other Family Members:
Spouse or Lover:
Friends' Names & Occupations:
Social Class:
Education:
Occupation/Employer:
Social Class:
Salary

Please contact me at jethompsonnovels@hushmail.com Request a blank character resume form and I will gladly email it to you.

IX Description: Be Extremely Specific!

Here are some thoughts about developing descriptions in your novels and short stories!

Be specific!

That's the clarion call to all creative writers as you pull your readers into your fictional dream. That's the reason description is considered an art form.

Description is simply a portrayal, in words, of something that can be perceived by the senses. Each time you use a word or phrase to describe a person, a setting or any other aspect of writing, it must be clear, concise and straight to the point, as it pertains to the situation.

As a writer, you are painting a word picture so the reader *sees* exactly what you are describing. It vividly portrays a person, place, or thing in such a way that the reader can visualize the topic and enter into the writer's experience or fictive dream.

Descriptive Goals as you write:

***Writer's create descriptions by using images with elaborate use of sensory language: Sight, sound, taste, feel, etc. It must be vivid.

***Writer's use figurative language such as simile, hyperbole, metaphor, symbolism and personification.

***Writer's use *Show, Don't Tell* through the use of active verbs and creative adjectives. When a writer really wants to go in depth in a scene, he or she will *show* as the mental movie rolls in the reader's mind. When the writer wants to get a quick point across or speed up a scene he will use *tell* in the scene.

Thoughts on Descriptive Writing:

• Make writing more concrete or vivid

• Add specific information

• Show sensory images

• Make comparisons

• Use dialogue

• Make writing more interesting

• Make characters come alive

Descriptive Writing Exercises:

Note: Keep a Descriptive Journal where you keep all your writing exercises. This will be a fantastic future reference to see your improvement as a writer.

1. Observe and then describe an event.

2. Walk outside your apartment or house and describe it in two ways:

a. *Tell:* Write a bare-bone version of the walk with few descriptions.

b. *Show*: Write a full-blown description of your walk with many descriptions: Use adjectives, descriptive phrases, metaphors, similes, etc.

c. Read each version out loud: You will see which version put the reader into the scene.

3. Reflect on a person or object that stands out in your memory. Write a description of that person/object.

4. Take a photograph, for example, and then describe the person, setting using the bare-bones approach, and then the full-blown approach.

X How to Write Subplots Without Losing the Reader!

How do you use subplots to your advantage in crafting a novel?

Have you ever driven down one of those winding backwoods roads in a rural area and couldn't figure out how to get back to the main highway? Well, that is the feeling a reader gets when they read a novel and get lost in a tangling subplot.

Your goal as an author is to create a little depth to your novel, maybe a little suspense, but not to take anything away from your main plot and pull your reader out of the "Fictive Dream" you worked so hard to create in the reader's mind.

What is a subplot?

***A subplot is a secondary plot that is supporting a side story for any story or main plot. Subplots may connect to main plots, in either time and place or in thematic significance. Subplots often involve supporting characters, those other than the protagonist or antagonist.

***Subplots can be distinguished from the main plot. They take up less of the action, less significant events occur within them, having a lesser impact on the book. Novels comment on one thing from multiple perspectives, with side trips here and there,

In a novel, you can take a side trip to provide extensive backstory or for other reasons. However, the subplot isn't really a side trip; it's a set of cohesive actions with its own main characters, goals, setbacks and resolutions.

Subplots are a sequence of events that parallels the main plot; it can closely resemble the main plot or it can diverge in significant ways in order to highlight the main plot.

Here is an example from my first novel, <u>A Brownstone in Brooklyn</u>... Jesse Towns and the possible horrific selling of the brownstone without the tenants knowledge was an early subplot. This subplot only took place during the first seven chapters, but it impacted the thematic development of the rest of the novel.

Key things to remember for all subplots!

1. They relate to the main plot and intersect with it in some way.

2. Don't swamp the main plot line with subplots. They must advance the story and help to show complexities in your characters.

Ideas for Subplots!

1. The main character can have more than one goal, usually relating to the main goal in some way.

2. Romantic subplots are common.

3. Secondary characters' concerns and goals. Perhaps one of the other characters is the hero of his/her own plot.

As you craft your novel, your objective is to pick and choose when to use subplots to add depth and possible suspense to your book. Subplots are most effective in the middle of a novel as the reader moves toward a hopefully climatic ending. Keep your readers on the main highway, but don't be afraid to make a detour to show a little extra scenery, fight some incredible battles or meet some new and interesting characters,

XI Scene Construction: This is the Difference Maker in a Successful Novel!

Novels are driven by incredible scene construction!

How a writer handles scenes will make the difference between a manuscript that sells, and one that ends up in the slush pile or the author receiving a rejection letter.

The scene is like a unit of drama in a novel.

The concept of a scene in fiction comes from theater, wherein it describes the action that takes place in a single setting.

The scene as we know it in modern genre fiction is heavily influenced by Hollywood. Life in the twenty-first century genre novel is a like series of quick, dramatic flashes.

When you flesh out a scene, you must either create a *show* scene or a *tell* scene to advance your storyline. This will affect your pacing. Be aware that you can speed up the action with *tell* scenes and slow it down with *show* scenes.

While writing A Brownstone in Brooklyn, I inserted a big *show* scene-sequence in the afternoon, with the evening being uneventful and nothing happening---a prelude—the riots in Brooklyn occurred the very next day.

You might wonder how I handled this sequence. I created tremendous *show* scenes depicting the day before the riots. I used *tell* scenes in the evening, but I created *show* scenes with specific sensory details the day of the riots.

The reader was forced into the moment and experienceds the riots as the flames ate away at the buildings on Nostrand Avenue in the Bedford-Stuyvesant section of Brooklyn. They smelled acrid smoke and saw the building crumble.

If I had created *show* scenes to flesh out the evening before the riot, I would be overwriting and would have slowed the novel down; the pacing would have been off mark.

When you create scenes with great *show/don't tell scenes* you want to do six things:

A. Possible Scene Format:

a. Scene One: Show Scene

b. Scene Two: Transition/Tell Scene

c. Scene Three: Show Scene

B. A scene has the following three-part pattern: Goal, Conflict and Disaster.

Goal: Your goal is to convincingly show your POV (Point OF View) Character experiencing the scene. (For Example, in the novel <u>To Kill A Mockingbird</u>, you are standing next to Atticus Finch as Tom Ewell spits in his face. You experience the spit dripping down Finch's face)

As you construct scenes, you must do this so powerfully that your reader experiences the scene as if he/she were the POV Character. Your reader will undeniably identify with the character.

Conflict: is the obstacles your POV character faces on the way to reaching his goal.

Disaster: is a failure to let your POV character reach his goal. Don't give him the goal without any conflict. Do Not Make It Easy!

C. A scene has three other important elements.

External Motivation: The objective can be in this paragraph. It does not need to be complicated.

Internal Motivation: *(the Internal scream):* Present it exactly as your POV character experiences it. This is your chance to make your reader be your POV character. (The character must have either an external or internal motivation---the reader must know why a character reacted a certain way.)

3. *Reflex Reaction*: It's instinctive. You will react rationally: to act, to think, to speak. You must present the full complexity of your character's reactions in this order.

For Example

EM: The man in black sprinted toward John flashing a switchblade.

IR: John turned, a bolt of raw adrenalin shot through his veins.

RR: John pulled a gun out of his shoulder holster, sighted on the man's chest, and squeezed the trigger, "You're dead!"

Key: You can't afford to write one scene, but you must write another scene, and another and another, etc. You will probably have to create hundreds of scenes before your book is complete.

(As a quick creative writing exercise--continue this scene)
AM (Another Motivation):
IR:
RR:

    I'm very interested in reading your continuation of this scene. What is John's next experience? Be specific---the reader must experience it and become part of John's reaction as he faces a man lunging at him with a switchblade!

    Please email comments, *jethompsonnovels@hushmail.com.*

XII. How Important is Good Grammar?

So...you've written a short story or a novel. You deserve a lot of credit. I bet you've worked very hard crafting your story. Do you remember that old saying, " The only things worth doing are worth doing right?" Would you agree with that? Are you shaking your head up and down? As an editor, I certainly am in agreement.

How important is good grammar? Sadly, many present-day writers believe that good grammar is not as important as a cohesive fast-paced story. When I edit, I have a few rules that I try to follow:

1) Be more or less specific.
2) Verbs has to agree with their subjects.
3) Contractions aren't always necessary and shouldn't be used to excess so don't.
4) Don't use no double negatives.

There are other rules I use. I chose these few to illustrate a point. Did you find these to be a bit humorous? If so, I have succeeded. Do these sound grammatically correct? How much credence would you have in your editor if he or she actually wrote like that?

Have you ever read a book written as poorly as the above? If so, did you actually finish it? I would have put it down after reading one paragraph. There is a simple method that I use to determine whether or not a sentence is grammatically correct and properly punctuated. I always read out loud, one word at a time.
If it doesn't sound right, it's not right.

How important is good grammar? I offer a bit of advice to our male readers/writers. This is crucial during the summer months. Never pee in a urinal with shorts on.

If you agree that good grammar is paramount, please take the time to read your story out loud and one word at a time. Pretend you are back in first grade. Touch each word with your index finger and say it aloud. I guarantee you will catch many things that you missed. You can take that to the bank and you will in the form of a much lower bill from your editor. Expect more five star reviews and increased sales as well. Good grammar rules!

XIII.   Editing Do's and Don'ts, Some Tricks and Tips

The Slow Turtle Wins the Race! That sounds corny but it's true. I have asked many writers one question. What would you change if you could do it all over again? Most responded with a short answer, "Slow down." Take time to look over your manuscript many times, from a writer's point of view, a reader's point of view and an editor's point of view. Do not be in a rush to send your manuscript to an editor or a publisher. Take time to edit your manuscript over and over. Let people read your manuscript, giving you pointers. Rewrite and reedit, let them read it again, until they are satisfied. Read it again slowly (remember what I said about first grade) until you are satisfied that you've done everything possible to make your manuscript the best it can be. Now, and only now, should you send your manuscript to an editor. Be smart, do a great job and reap the benefit of a much lower bill at the end of the process, one that you can afford and be happy with.

The Slow Turtle says: "Have your book edited by a professional!" ... Have you ever seen a book that was poorly edited? Do you enjoy reading books that are not edited well? I have seen many books riddled with punctuation errors, misspelled words, helter-skelter organization, formatting issues and disjointed action.

Does that measure up to your writing standard? Do you feel comfortable publishing something that you put a lot of effort into without having it edited by a professional? Very few writers can edit their own work. I have met and talked to hundreds of writers in the last six plus years. Based on my editing standard, I only know one writer that has done a fantastic job editing his own work.

I strongly suggest that you plan to have your story or novel edited by a professional. Select your editor very carefully. Take the time to get to know each other. Perhaps you can meet face-to-face, if not, talk at length on the telephone. E-mail is not the best means of communication. Work very closely with your editor; take the time to become a *writing team* in order to make your book or short story the best it can be.

The Slow Turtle says: "Choose your publisher carefully!"

Do not choose the first publisher you see on the net when you are ready to find one. If you do, you will pay in the long run, perhaps thousands of dollars before you even see a galley copy.

Take the time to make a list of publishers that you think might be compatible with your piece of fiction. While making a list, refer to these resources to help you make good choices:

1) **Editors and Predators** has a lengthy list of publishers, evaluating each one truthfully.
2) **BBB.org**- You can search within a state or zip code for Better Business Bureau accredited publishers or those not accredited. Of course, some publishers will have more complaints listed than others, based on their size.
3) **Ripoffreport.com**- another informative site, including much more than just publishers.

Most publishers want your money. Should you have to pay to have a book published? You can, if you are willing, do much of the work yourself. I have searched long and hard looking for those publishers that ask for no money up front. They do exist; I have found a few and I will gladly share that information with you, should you care to e-mail me.

Whether you decide to self-publish or use a traditional publisher, please be very very careful. Take your time and make a wise decision. Good research will pay off in the long run. *If you have any questions about editing, publishing or marketing, please contact Julius or myself. We are here to help you. I wish you the best of luck on your writing journey.*

Bonus Thoughts

for Authors!

The Elements of a Successful 21st Century Author!

Successful twenty-first century authors have three lifestyle components: Passion, Organization, and Uniqueness.

Passion: Successful authors love their craft!

They delve into the storyline with abandon. They make time to write and know their most creative time of the day. This is different for each author.

I know a writer who sneaks out of bed at four a.m. and writes until six a.m. and then returns to bed and the warmth of his spouse.

In the space between daily tasks writers will find a time to write. I'm a high school teacher and sometimes, in the six minutes between classes, I will have a pencil and pad in the hallway and in between yelling "Get to Class!" I can write a few lines for an upcoming manuscript.

Later, after the closing school bells sounds, I expand on my recent idea and thought and make it into something that is readable. Write whenever and wherever you can!

The health of a writer's soul must be nurtured and developed.

Successful authors find the time to write, creating that *"next"* new and exciting scene in their novel.

Organization: Successful writers...Write!

They write story lines. They write chapters. They outline. They jot down notes for their books. They are on schedule with dates of submissions and deadlines, constantly jostling their brain cells.

Successful writers use technology, old and new. From pen and paper, to a laptop or a PC. Dictionary.com accounts, thesaurus, smart authors have everything at arm's length, situated neatly at their writing station.

They write!

I use an android to keep a schedule of my writing. I have chapters organized, complete with one and two notes about what I want to accomplish in the writing of that particular chapter.

I have two android folders:

***One folder contains all the chapters listed and the particular notes, setting and dialogue that fits that particular moment in the novel.

The other folder contains the entire novel. When I finish a chapter in one folder, I copy/paste that chapter into the novel folder. As the chapters build, I can keep an eye see on the word count and get a feel and flow in the storyline.

These two folders give me the opportunity and freedom to work in one folder and keep a completed version in another folder.

Folder One: Each individual chapter word document is listed 1-to 50 with all the incomplete chapters.

Folder Two: The entire novel. As I complete a chapter, I add that chapter to it, slowly building the first draft.

Currently, I'm working on Chapter Seven in **Stormy Winds**!

Uniqueness: Successful writers have their own voice, pacing, and storyline.

They are not robots.

They do not write in trendy categories, popular genres or alter themes to suit the masses. However, some writers do. For me, I want to be unique and different.

Unique writers write the story they want to tell and let the world know how they feel.

They are creative.

Regardless of our reasons for pulling a chair into a comfortable position in front of a computer and writing, we measure success by finishing what we started!

Is Finding a literary Agent an impossible task?

Never Give Up On Your Dream!

I imagine myself sitting in front of my computer slapping my head from side to side...Finding an agent is so difficult that, at times you might want to slap your head from side to side until you have forgotten our own name.

Maybe, if I slap hard enough my brain will work in overdrive to figure out a way to get agents interested in my fifth novel: Stormy Winds.

I feel like Don Quixote of La Mancha, chasing the Impossible Dream.

What a process!

I have several well-grounded qualifications:

***Four published novels: A Brownstone in Brooklyn, Philly Style and Philly Profile, The Ghost of Atlanta and Phantoms of Rockwood.

***2007, 2011 and 2014 Georgia of the Year nominations.

***My third novel, The Ghost of Atlanta, won Reader's Favorite 2011 National Gold Medal for General Fiction!

*** The Ghost of Atlanta is on the Barnes & Nobles bookshelves, currently in small libraries and is selling at a good pace. That's right, on the book shelves of nation-wide Barnes & Nobles Bookstores.

***I've been a presenter at the 2009 AJC-Decatur Book Festival in Decatur, Georgia, the 2010 Virginia Festival of the Book in Charlottesville, Virginia and the 2010 Buffalo Book Fair in Buffalo, New York.

*** I work hard at building a platform for my books and have managed to scale many marketing barriers. I will work even harder, jumping many hurdles to reach my goal of becoming a well-known author.

***I'm a former creative writing instructor at Evening and Emory in Atlanta, Georgia.

*** I have a fantastic editor, Dennis DeRose, and I searched ten long years to find him.

Yet, all of my writing accomplishments seems invisible to agents.

I work hard at writing my novels and I'm extremely dedicated in marketing.

However, frustration sets in at times and erodes my enthusiasm.

I read something on agent Linda Roghaar's website a comment that works like an aspirin to eases the pain:

"Don't take rejection personally. More often than not a rejection is not about your writing; you've gotten it to the wrong person at the wrong time. Look at the package critically and send it out to another agent."

Yet the agent front is silent for me...totally void of a positive response.

I've followed all the rules, my four published books are well received and have garnered national honors and recognition, but I keep getting the following form letter:

Dear Author:

Thank you so much for sending the (Blank) Literary Agency your query. We'd like to apologize for the impersonal nature of this standard rejection letter. Rest assured that we do read every query letter carefully and, unfortunately, this project is not right for us. Because this business is so subjective and opinions vary widely, we recommend that you pursue other agents. After all, it just takes one "yes" to find the right match.

Good luck with all your publishing endeavors.

Well, I'll just keep sending out query letters and hopefully I'll find that one agent who will say *"Yes."*

Ooh...my aching head!

Do One Thing Every Day That Scares You!

You must take chances to achieve your dreams!

You Must Take Chances in life to reach your goals!

I can't believe I waited until the autumn years of my life to take on this risky business!

For the first time in my life, not too long ago, I stepped of my box, taking on a big challenge, a video blog about writing confidence. I had to face the camera and express my feelings in public. That was an exhilarating experience.

Now, I've developed an interactive website with funky music (developed my Donald Moody II), videos and audio readings of certain chapters of Philly Style and Philly Profile.

I was nervous about the Video Blog, you can catch it on YouTube. It is receiving positive recognition.

My new twenty-first Century Website, with all the flash, colorful images and sounds, is enough to drive a person out of middle age.

I feel this is the next big step in the marketing of my books: A Brownstone in Brooklyn, Philly Style and Philly Profile, The Ghost of Atlanta, Phantoms of Rockwood, and the soon to be published Stormy Winds.

I remember what Eleanor Roosevelt once said: "Do one thing every day that scares you."

You better believe I'm scared!

However, that is what life is about: Growth and Change and Ultimate Success

Don't be afraid to step out of the box abandon your comfort zone.

Dennis, my editor, and I are both here for you. Feel free to contact us with any questions or comments. Please send comments to jethompsonnovels@hushmail.com or on twitter @jethompsone1. Dennis DeRose can be reached at ddrose@hvc.rr.com .

---30---

DEDICATION

Ms. Francis Grief my Special friend in Heaven!

www.ingramcontent.com/pod-product-compliance
Lightning Source LLC
Chambersburg PA
CBHW070339290526
45791CB00003B/1402